<u>Note</u>
This booklet's information came from the author's education and experiences with criminals and crime victims. It is intended to assist in recovery from trauma of all origins.

Evolutionary Emotional Intelligence: Redefining PTSD

by
Boyd Patterson, M.A., J.D.

For A.R.

"This book breaks things down into logical, practical and objective terms for those who have experienced trauma in their lives, regardless of the type. Mr. Patterson provides victims another coping tool that helps them recognize exactly what they are experiencing, step back, analyze and deescalate themselves."
Amy Griffin, RN
Former Nursing Director
Rape Crisis Center

"This book is an excellent guide for helping individuals accurately define PTSD and its therapeutic communication."
Ronnie Boyd
Retired combat veteran and counselor

"This book gives a short, well laid out definition of PTSD, giving voice to unanswered questions asked by people battling PTSD. Staying in the present and inquiring about these struggles builds healthier patterns away from fear and toward empowerment and thriving. This book is a great tool to this end."
Brian Stoddard, LPC
Trauma Focused Cognitive Behavioral Therapist

Table of Contents

Part I: The Foundation of
Emotional Stability

One more life-preserver

As a trauma survivor, you know all too well the intense feelings associated with Post-Traumatic Stress Disorder (PTSD). They rise like tidal waves and crash into your day, washing away self-control. In those moments of sudden crisis, helpful information about PTSD acts like a life preserver. Knowledge will not prevent the emotional waves from occurring, but can help you weather the storm. Such increased awareness often comes from therapists, fellow survivors and recovery literature. This small booklet represents these tiny steps of progress available to you at all times. Even a slight increase in understanding about your condition can help you stay more grounded (or less distressed) during hyper-vigilance and flashbacks.

As a counselor, I recognized that human emotions flow from the evolved instincts we all possess. Nearly two decades of working in the criminal justice system confirmed that those primitive instincts fuel most of our destructive and self-destructive tendencies. Trauma activates these core-level survival drives, regularly afflicting both criminals and crime victims with PTSD.

Fortunately, modern science recognizes the condition's biological nature, similar in many ways to other common physical injuries. A broken bone and PTSD both come from severe trauma. Both cause extremely uncomfortable bodily sensations. With an informed treatment plan, proper 'framing' of the injury, painstaking rehabilitation and patience, both types of patients can legitimately hope to recover.

Understanding PTSD as a physiological condition may strike you as unusual.

However, scientists across the world now attest to the condition's biological and neurochemical aspects. In fact, the day is probably near when trauma survivors will say "I had PTSD" in the same context others say "I had a broken arm."

This booklet integrates several recovery techniques, many of which you may already know. Recognizing PTSD as a <u>physical</u> condition constitutes the foundation of this treatment approach. Your journey will likely involve collecting additional insights and experiences. Hopefully, like a life preserver, some of the information in these pages can add to your emotional stability during surges of distress.

<u>Getting stable</u>

When struggling with a confusing situation, perhaps the most stability

comes from *defining the problem.*
Consider the history of how clinicians
learned to treat PTSD. As you might
know, traumatic stress has affected
human beings for millennia. It was only
about 100 years ago, when large groups
of former soldiers started returning
home from war, that clinicians started
developing a definition of this common
condition. The initial terms "shell
shock" and "battle fatigue" gave way to
the more fitting diagnostic term "post-
traumatic stress disorder." Today's well-
established clinical definition of PTSD
helps treatment providers by describing
common symptoms and root causes,
thus indicating steps to recovery.

Unfortunately, most survivors remain
as baffled about PTSD recovery as
clinicians were a hundred years ago.
The symptoms keep your head
spinning with fear. Perpetually
blindsided, you can never really get

your bearings. Thankfully, like modern day clinicians, you too can benefit from a stabilizing definition of PTSD. The simple definition in this booklet uses *non*-clinical terms to describe your symptoms, root causes and steps to recovery.

Ideally, this new "survivor-centric" definition will provide the same therapeutic stability to you and other survivors as the clinical definition provides to therapists. When stunned by the overwhelming emotions, you no longer wonder what hit you. The definition explains the situation. This stable life preserver allows you to remain more objective during hyper-vigilance. You can accept the signs of an imminent panic attack and simply focus on making yourself as comfortable as possible. You can recognize during a flashback that, like riding a roller coaster or watching a movie, it's just a chemical experience that will end.

Every organism naturally moves toward balanced relaxation, i.e., homeostasis. Sooner or later, you *will* reacquire emotional stability. Your challenge rests in remaining patient while your brain gradually recovers. The following definition of PTSD facilitates this restoration by providing a stable understanding of the condition, using terms survivors can embrace.

<u>A survivor's definition</u>

For our purposes, we define PTSD as:

**1) Chemically-induced tunnel vision
2) caused by fused neural pathways
3) that can be realigned.**

This three-part definition frames the condition in non-clinical terms that all survivors can understand. Just as therapists use the clinical definition as the foundation of their PTSD practice, you can use the non-clinical definition as the foundation of your recovery. It describes PTSD from the common survivor perception of feeling "stuck." So consider your PTSD as being:

1) stuck in the tunnel vision of fear;
2) because actual neural pathways in your brain, fused by trauma, remain *physically* stuck together;
3) which can be realigned back into healthy, diverse neural pathways.

As you apply this definition during times of crisis, feel free to modify the words to better fit your personal experience. So you can better recognize the driving terror of a flashback for its true nature: **chemicals.** Chemicals that create uncomfortable body sensations and a **tunnel vision** of "threat." Tunnel vision that hides the positive aspects of your surroundings from view. All caused by **fused neural pathways** in your brain, seared together during your traumatic experience. Pathways that can be **realigned** back into healthy, diverse neural formations.

Ultimately, we want to restore your emotional versatility, which leads to emotional freedom. So you can once again recognize the full range of environmental stimuli and respond with the full range of appropriate emotions. In time, we will reduce your traumatic experience to just one more chapter of your overall life story. Your psyche's shattered pieces will realign into one cohesive whole. And your PTSD will shift to PTSO: Post-Traumatic Stress *Order*.

As earlier stated, we will consider trauma solely in the context of its physical impact upon your brain. The next section describes how a healthy brain functions. Ideally, this will remind you of your pre-trauma mental state and start tugging you out of feeling emotionally stuck in the past.

<u>Mental versatility</u>

In many ways, your brain operates as a computer:

Input ---> Process ---> Output

<u>Input</u>: like a keyboard sending type-written data to your computer's central processing unit, your sensory organs (eyes, ears, skin, etc.) send information about sight, sound, temperature, etc. to your brain.

<u>Process</u>: just as your computer's CPU processes received data, your brain

processes the input received from the environment.

<u>Output</u>: computer CPUs send out electronic output based on the processed data. Likewise, your brain releases neurochemicals based upon the processed information about your environment. Again:

Environmental <u>Input</u> leads to
Neural <u>Processing</u> that triggers
Emotional-Chemical <u>Output</u>.

Healthy brains release neurochemicals that accurately correspond to the circumstances of the environment. <u>Key concept</u>: once the environment provides *different* input, a healthy brain releases *different* chemicals, which create *different* emotions. See a beautiful sunrise? A healthy brain releases chemicals that create feelings of wonder. Later argue with a hostile co-worker? That brain releases different chemicals that create proportionate feelings of threat. Still later read a positive email from your supervisor? That brain releases still different chemicals that create feelings of accomplishment.

For PTSD recovery purposes, the takeaway: a healthy brain remains versatile, recognizing the changes in the environment and activating the neural pathways that best respond to the changing circumstances.

Regaining this ability to change mental gears constitutes our goal for you. The emotional tidal waves may rise and fall, but your recovery goal remains stable. You possessed great versatility before the trauma, appropriately responding to changes in your surroundings. Recognize your countless pre-trauma experiences involving several different

emotions as recovery assets. Then
acknowledge that regaining such
emotional versatility is possible. As you
will discover, consistent progress
toward this goal flows from recognizing
PTSD as:

1) **Chemically-induced tunnel vision**
2) **caused by fused neural pathways**
3) **that can be realigned.**

Let us now examine the three
components of our definition.

Part II: Understanding The Three Components

1) <u>Chemically-induced tunnel vision</u>

This first component defines the mental gear designed to address dire physical threat. When the environment indicates extreme danger, your brain automatically activates the survival-related neural pathways, otherwise known as the sympathetic nervous system. Adrenaline, norepinephrine and cortisol flood your body, producing the physical sensations of emotions. These chemicals facilitate "fight-flight-freeze-collapse" behaviors, increasing your heartbeat, dumping glucose into your bloodstream, quickening your reflexes and dulling your sense of pain.

As a result, you see the world through **chemically-induced tunnel vision,** focused upon a potential threat, ignoring anything unrelated to that threat. When the threat passes, your brain shifts gears and activates the neural pathways that facilitate recovery, known as the parasympathetic nervous system. Relaxing brain chemicals such as serotonin and GABA flush out the threat-related chemicals, eventually transitioning you back to balanced relaxation. Shifting mental gears from one extreme to another takes time but, again, a healthy brain retains such versatility, matching your emotions to the changing environment.

Traumatic stress destroys that versatility, keeping you stuck in the gear of fear. Long after the threat passes, the "fight-flight-freeze-collapse" chemicals still course through your system. Your body remains tense, braced for catastrophe. Even when you cognitively understand no threat exists, the chemicals maintain the fear-related tunnel vision. You remain blind to the positive aspects of your situation. Your tunnel vision sees only danger, forcing you to constantly scan the environment for threats. It's not rational; it's chemical.

Yet even in that chemically-induced state of fear, it *is* possible to recognize that, indeed, it's just the chemicals talking. You cannot ignore them (no one can), but seeing the chemicals' true nature takes the edge off the experience. With patience, you will see that no actual threat exists, merely a chemically-induced perception of threat. There's no need to fight, flee, freeze or collapse, only a chemically-induced push to do so. An incredibly powerful hoax, but still a hoax. Over time, repeated instances of such recognition start pulling the tunnel vision apart, increasing your mental stability during times of crisis. The mountainous emotional waves may still turn your stomach, but you can better ride them out clinging to the recognition that "it's just chemicals."

Some survivors keep a list of things to remember during a flashback. If you keep such a list, add to it the survivor-oriented definition of PTSD. Accept the chemically-induced tunnel vision as the most amazing hoax you've ever experienced. Keep reminding yourself that the "danger chemicals" in your body pose no danger themselves. And they always pass. Knowing this will hopefully keep your head above water during the blinding storm.

PTSD

1) Chemically-induced tunnel vision
2) <u>**caused by fused neural pathways**</u>

In July of 2016, a bolt of lightning struck my house and fried the electrical circuit panel. Some of the wiring remained unaffected; other wires melted together.

We salvaged some electrical appliances and had to replace others. Disruptive and annoying, but nothing personal. It simply meant filling out some insurance forms and, eventually, hiring an electrician to dig through and realign the mess of damaged wiring.

Think of your brain as your body's main circuit panel. Operating properly, the circuits send power to many different areas of your body. Before your traumatic event, your brain flexibly responded to various situations by routing electrochemical energy down the appropriate wires, i.e., nerve pathways.

Now consider a scientific truth, accepted as fact by every neuroscientist on the planet: intense experiences fuse neural pathways together. Simply put: *the neurons that fire together wire together.* Like the lightning bolt that fried my house's circuits, your intense trauma fused the "fight-flight-freeze-collapse" pathways in your brain together with other neural pathways. In other words, you took a massive electrochemical bolt of trauma (input). It overloaded the threat-response pathways in your brain, melting them together with the other 'wires' in your main circuit panel (processing). Now, almost every kind of environmental input stimulates that fused bundle of nerves, automatically releasing the fight-flight-freeze-collapse chemicals (output). Emotional jolts **caused by fused neural pathways.**

As a result, you move through life stuck in one gear, regardless of the input's nature. See that beautiful sunrise? Your shocked brain maintains the tunnel vision of threat. Argue with that hostile co-worker? Your shocked brain maintains the tunnel vision of threat. Read that positive email from your supervisor? Your shocked brain stubbornly maintains the tunnel vision of threat. Zero mental versatility. Although you feel great physical discomfort, again, this condition is truly nothing personal. The stomach knots, chest tightness, weak knees, etc., all flow from microscopically-tiny fused 'wires' in your brain, sending signals of threat when no threat exists.

Understanding the symptoms' root cause as a *physical* wiring issue makes the bodily discomfort more objective. An emotional lightning strike over-loaded a neural circuit, fusing some wires together; disruptive and annoying, but nothing personal. PTSD isn't a good thing or a bad thing. It's just a survival response, designed by evolution to keep us alive during life-threatening situations.

Of course, understanding the neutral nature of brain cell adhesions doesn't mean you won't get zapped with a flashback. However, you can recognize during moments of crisis that the emotions all flow from a tiny bundle of fused nerves. This recognition allows you to accept the physical symptoms as coming from a neutral source, just as you would accept discomfort from a broken bone as it heals.

Acknowledging PTSD simply as fused nerves reduces your distress, giving you the extra mental space necessary to start healing. It also fits perfectly with an effective therapeutic technique: using increased awareness to pull those stuck wires back apart. Which brings us to the third component of our definition.

PTSD
1) Chemically-induced tunnel vision
2) caused by fused neural pathways
3) **that can be realigned**.

As earlier described, PTSD shares similarities with fused wiring. So try to visualize the trauma-fused pathway in your brain. Picture that little nerve cluster as it routes electrochemical energy to different areas of your body, creating false alarm and physical discomfort. To heal, visualize those neural adhesions getting pulled back apart. Imagine the single fused pathway realigning back into multiple healthy circuits, selectively channeling energy without triggering the "fight-flight-freeze-collapse" chemicals. Our primary technique for this task: distraction.

As a young counselor, I questioned distraction's usefulness as a therapeutic tool. To me, distraction meant looking away from the problem, thus avoiding what needed to be confronted. Later came a compelling demonstration of Eye Movement Desensitization and Reprocessing (EMDR), a distraction technique often used on military veterans. After observing how EMDR significantly reduced PTSD's physical symptoms, I embraced distraction's effectiveness regarding PTSD recovery.

Consider also the relevant root words. "Tract" basically means "pathway," such as the neural pathways in your brain. You now know that your trauma fused several of those pathways together; by intensely firing together they wired together. This fused bundle of nerves constitutes a tangled new pathway, i.e., "tract," that triggers your destabilizing emotional surges.

For purposes of recovery, dis-traction means separating that fused tangle back into its various original neural pathways. Prying back apart its separate filaments, microfiber by microfiber. <u>Key concept</u>: intentionally directing your attention to different aspects of your surroundings *physically* activates different areas of your brain. Bringing these multiple neural pathways back online starts getting your fused neural pathways "unstuck." Put another way: freeing neural adhesions frees your positive emotions. Gradually, this process starts rerouting electrochemical energy back along the proper routes. Hence the recovery aspect of our definition of PTSD: fused neural pathways **that can be realigned.**

You may initially consider distraction techniques inadequate to resolve your enormous emotions. Overwhelming anxiety often drives survivors to seek more immediate solutions to their discomfort. To self-medicate for instant relief. To value only great therapeutic breakthroughs. To just "snap out of it." However, PTSD recovery is a process, accessible to you *right now* within every tiny therapeutic gain. The way ocean currents gradually shift the sands over time, grain by grain. The way a budding leaf creeps forward throughout the Spring.

Don't get duped by the tunnel vision's illusion that you must immediately overcome your trauma. Remember that any emotional urgency to "snap out of it" flows from a chemical hoax. No actual threat exists anymore. Therefore, nothing bad will happen by dropping your guard to heal. A real path to recovery lies under your feet right now; it's just a slow one. As risky as it feels, accept and trust the *gradual* nature of PTSD recovery. Value small victories and, thus, take a big step forward in your healing process.

Part III: Meditation for Recovery

<u>Realignment through distraction</u>

Mindfulness meditation remains one of the most useful tools for PTSD recovery. The process generally involves creating a healthy mindset by guiding your awareness toward subtle aspects of your surroundings. Gentle shifts of attention naturally shift your other mental gears back into action. Mindfully focusing on your breathing, or the pressure of a chair seat, or the sounds around you, (re)engages multiple neural pathways. Paying attention in the present moment, without judgment, opens that fused bundle, dis-tracting the nerve fibers apart, thread by tiny thread.

Directing your awareness toward the various details around you softly tugs at those shocked pathways. Electro-chemical energy gets redirected out of the charred wad of the past and back into the present moment. Even the smallest of these distractions helps free the 'threat pathways' from the 'non-threat pathways.' Daily meditation that gently transitions through numerous positive mindsets gradually restores your cognitive versatility, moving you back towards the automatic shifting of mental gears in response to environmental changes. And the best part about meditation: *it feels good while you do it.*

Additionally, you will discover when building your practice that taking smaller steps produces greater gains. Meditation works by helping you take tiny steps every day toward brain recovery. Paying close attention without judgment...to sunlight warming your skin...a bird's melody...the sharp taste of a fresh orange...delicately pulls apart the filaments of your trauma-fused neural pathways. Bit by bit. Cell by cell.

As the therapeutic saying goes: "progress over perfection." Almost every bit of mindful progress brings a small drop of physical relief.

As a recovery tool, meditation supports more primary treatment approaches, including EMDR and cognitive-behavioral therapy (CBT). Prolonged Exposure therapy dis-tracts traumatic memories by you facing them while remaining grounded in the present moment. Cognitive Processing pulls traumatic memories apart by expanding your limited perspective about them. Meditation facilitates these therapies by increasing your overall awareness. Every meditation session involves observing the smallest nuances of your breathing, surroundings and flow of thoughts. All without judgment. Understand that your trauma-related emotions will probably flare up during meditation, as they do during other parts of your day. No problem, for our goal isn't perfect meditative focus. In fact, we need not "achieve" any particular mindset. Seeking a better mindset, even wanting to seek it, also moves us forward.

So when the chemicals/emotions flare up during meditation, ride them out. After they pass (again they always pass), redirect your attention toward the intended healthy mindset. Expect your mind to drift during meditation. Remember: the specific neural adhesions pulling your attention away from your meditation mindset can themselves be dis-tracted. Achieve this by gently guiding your attention back to the intended mindset. If you often struggle to maintain focus, your expectations may be too great. Reduce them. As you meditate, simply value a positive mindset and feel what happens. Little by little, seeking emotional health

moves you closer to actually obtaining
it.

<u>Basic Meditation</u>

Try the following exercise. When you
get 10-20 minutes of free time, find a
quiet space where you can comfortably
sit. You can close your eyes or keep
them open. When ready, take a deep
breath. Then more slowly take another.
Then one more, even slower. And
then...

*Notice the pressure of the chair pushing up
against you...Feel the support of the chair
back...The ground touching your feet...
Feel your hands resting on your lap...Do
not actively listen; let sounds come to
you...Do not assign meaning to the
sensations; simply accept them. No judging
or interpreting. Just sensing.*

*Pay attention to your breath. Notice the
rise and fall of your stomach...The sound of*

your breathing...The cool air passing over your upper lip during the inhale...The inner pressure in your stomach as the inhale peaks...The warmer air of your exhale... Don't change anything about your breathing; just observe...If your mind drifts, gently bring your attention back to your breathing as it happens.

Now allow your mind to wander...Notice your drifting thoughts...Let them fully surface into your awareness, but do nothing in response...Accept your thoughts without judgment, as they flow...Leaves floating by on a stream...Do nothing...For there is nothing to do...Like watching a wadded rubber band unravel itself...Just let it happen.

Pay attention to your random thoughts, until new thoughts drift into your awareness...Allow the old thoughts to naturally fade away...Let the past go and, soon enough, the past will let go of you.

Somewhere in that exercise I hope you experienced at least a small bit of peace. Find the right meditation method and you will discover that every mindful shift of attention effects a microscopic distraction of fused nerves. Which brings a moment of blessed relief. Perhaps record the words of the previous exercise into an audio file, in your own voice, then listen when you find quiet time. Definitely seek out different sources of meditation instruction. Your therapist can likely provide some direction. A meditation group probably meets in your area. Explore mindfulness videos on YouTube. Smartphone apps such as Headspace and Breathe2Relax cost a little money, but provide structured exercises designed to start realigning those fused neural pathways.

<u>Mindfulness for
uncomfortable physical sensations</u>

When PTSD manifests as disruptive body sensations, the five observation techniques described below can pull your attention away from the discomfort. They reframe your perspective about the sensations, helping peel the "stuck" neural pathways back apart one nerve cell at a time. If you prefer utilizing a consistent routine, cycle through the techniques in the order listed below. However, many survivors prefer novel applications. So when the physical symptoms twist up your gut, chest, head, etc., consider jumping from technique to technique in random order.

1. <u>Acknowledge the sensation.</u> Quit trying to ignore the feeling. We want to increase your awareness about the biochemical hoax getting perpetrated

upon you. Acknowledging the physical sensation helps shift your vantage point more toward observation. Perhaps even curiosity. Maintaining objectivity about the feeling creates a tiny bit of separation from it, which keeps you more stable.

2. <u>Accept the sensation</u>. Don't fight or resist it anymore. The false sense of danger emanates from very real neuro-chemicals, which evolved for a purpose: facilitating survival behaviors relevant to the harsh environment of our ancestors. Fighting a rival. Fleeing mortal danger. Freezing to avoid detection. Collapsing to survive an overwhelming force. All while hypervigilence keeps you braced for catastrophic threat.

Accepting the emotional waves allows them to pass through your body *without acting out the primitive behaviors.* So accept the physical feelings, while doing nothing about them. Recovery literature encourages addicts to sometimes "let go and let God" handle their problems. You can do the same with uncomfortable physical sensations. Simply observe them as they shift and change form. Let the emotions naturally unwind. Ride them out until they dissipate. Stop fighting the feelings and they will stop fighting with you.

3. <u>Analyze the sensation</u>. Recognize the physical sensation as one more "energy mode" emanating from your brain. Just as an electrician inspects fused wiring in a house, you can objectively explore the electrochemical energy moving through your nerve pathways. Be curious about the bodily sensations. Examine their nuances. Where specific-ally in your stomach/chest/head does the sensation exist? How deep does it

go? Does it have a shape? Does it move?
What specific sensation does it
produce? Don't try to change the
feeling; just observe it. Remember that
the emotion isn't good or bad; it's just
outdated wiring designed to make your
genes successful.

4. <u>Remember that other emotions exist</u>.
Even though the uncomfortable
physical symptoms dominate your
current awareness, they represent a tiny
fraction of your feelings. Remember
your emotional versatility before the
trauma. You once experienced a variety
of physiological sensations, positive and
negative, as responses to a variety of life
circumstances. That wide range of
emotional possibilities still exists within
you. Recognize the real existence of
those other mental gears, currently
hidden by the tunnel vision of PTSD.
Start cracking apart the blinders by
acknowledging that fear constitutes just

one emotional mode of many in your existing collection.

5. <u>Redirect the sensation's energy</u>. You didn't ask to be stuck in these feelings; they basically fell from the sky upon you. Now forced to deal with them, you might as well discharge their energy into productive activities. That seething emotion drives action. So go ahead and act, but in a direction of your choosing. Yard work. Exercise. Even menial household tasks all provide opportunities to practice discharging the energy in productive ways. If the physical sensations flare up at work, find some aspect of your job into which you can channel the emotions. I never lacked motivation when prosecuting criminals who preyed upon minors. Likewise, you can appropriately express your trauma-related feelings through work projects. Our evolved instincts have outlived the brutal environment

that shaped them. However, by reframing our perspectives about emotions, we can direct them toward productive action.

Knowing that you possess a variety of responses in your emergency toolbox can help reduce the intensity and frequency of the physical sensations. Daily meditation transitions you through multiple mindsets, adding several healthy perspectives to your toolbox as well. <u>Practice tip</u>: do not expect this process to immediately make the uncomfortable feelings go away. Instead, hope for the *smallest* level of dis-traction away from the feeling. Then *further* reduce that miniscule expectation. Next take away any expectation and replace it with a mere *value* of therapeutic progress. Finally, simply appreciate the fact that therapeutic progress *might* occur someday. Then get ready to discover something wonderful about how reducing your expectations reduces your physical discomfort in the moment.

Redefining PTSD provides one more life-preserver

We often forget that taking tiny steps forward *still moves us forward*. The slightest observations experienced in daily meditation will gently pull apart and restore your charred neural pathways. Mindful observation is one technique of many. Other recovery tools such as deep breathing, guided imagery and (strangely) counting backwards by sevens also operate to dis-tract your tiny fused bundle, if only slightly. Seek to accumulate small therapeutic gains and you will find that, on this journey, less is truly more. Even on bad days, you can take comfort in the fact that you possess recovery tools with proven effectiveness. And on good days you get a taste of the more lasting relief that awaits.

I hope that the PTSD definition for survivors provides you with greater emotional stability, just as the clinical definition provides therapists with greater clinical stability. Getting unstuck takes time, but will happen for you. So remain patient and let the shattered pieces weave themselves back together. This definition can establish a solid foundation for all future recovery efforts. And in time you will personally experience the ultimate freedom from trauma: *gratitude,* which leads to forgiveness of yourself, and of others.

Finally, if you re-read this booklet, you will realize how the three aspects of our "survivor-centric" definition connect PTSD's:

1) Symptoms,
2) Root causes and
3) Steps to recovery.

So try recognizing:

1) **Chemically-induced tunnel vision** *as your symptom(s),*
2) **Fused neural pathways** *as the physical cause of your condition and*
3) **Realigning** *them through distraction as one more path to recovery.*

Keep paddling, my friend.

Boyd Patterson has studied crime and psychology for over two decades, serving in several roles within the criminal justice system. He received his Bachelor's and Master's degrees in psychology and counseled delinquent youth, many of whom had been victimized. As a prosecutor, he worked with survivors of child abuse, sexual assault and domestic violence. As Gang Task Force Coordinator, Mr. Patterson worked with youth at risk of joining gangs, focusing on those regularly exposed to traumatic stress. He has served as a Children's Advocacy Center board member, Mental Health Court steering committee member and Rape Crisis Center volunteer. Mr. Patterson currently works as an Assistant Public Defender, representing indigent criminal defendants, many of whom suffer from PTSD.